FROM THE ASHES

A Memoir

CLIFF HALL SR.

abbott press

Abbott Press books may be ordered through booksellers or by contacting:

Abbott Press
1663 Liberty Drive
Bloomington, IN 47403
www.abbottpress.com
Phone: 1 (866) 697-5310

ISBN: 978-1-4582-2081-3 (sc)
ISBN: 978-1-4582-2080-6 (e)

Library of Congress Control Number: 2017900464

Print information available on the last page.

Abbott Press rev. date: 02/28/2017

Contents

From the Ashes

Clint's heart was in his throat as he stood watching his house burn to the ground. Even at the age of six he knew that *this* moment would affect his life in the future.

But let's start at the beginning:

Clint was born on a small farm in Appling County, Georgia. In the town of Baxley. The year was 1930 and it was the start of the Great Depression. He was the second of what would eventually become nine children. Eight boys and one girl.

The fire began on the back porch where on of Clint's Younger brothers was playing with matches. He accidently set fire to the fodder (husks stripped from corn stalks). They were bundled and left on the porch to dry to make animal food. Conyer, the one who started the fire, came into the house and told his mother there was smoke on the back porch. At first Eva, his mom, and Edward his eldest brother, tried to put out the fire with water from the well. However, the fire started to spread. Eva sent Clint to another house, about ¼ mile down the road to get help from his Uncle Staten. When Uncle Staten and Clint returned, all they could do was watch as the roof caved in on the family home.

At the time, Clint was unaware that his mother had nearly lost her life in the fire. Eva and Edward had been trying to bring some of the furniture out of the house. They had gotten as far as the front gate when Eva remembered she had laid the baby on the bed. She dashed back into the house only to see the mattress engulfed in flames. In her mind, she imagined she saw the baby laying on the mattress. In a frightened state of shock, she grabbed a hold of the door frame, which was already on fire screaming, *"My baby! My Baby!"*

When Edward saw his mother run back into the burning house, he ran after her and pulled her out into the front yard. Stripped off her sweater that has caught fire when she grabbed the door frame. Despite the fact she was later shown the baby, who was unharmed. Eva was in such a state of shock that she refused believe the child was hers. It took several days before she accepted the fact that her baby was indeed alive and well.

Clint's father had gone to work earlier that morning. The children were getting ready for school when the fire broke out. The school was a one room school house where the teacher taught grades one through three.

After their home burned down it was the beginning of a long and uncertain future. This event however, would take Clint from being the son of a small farmer to one day being vice president of a large company.

For a while, the family moved in and lived with their Grandmother. Before long Aaren, his father decided to move the family about 45 miles south to Waycross, G.A. Aaren was always looking for work or a way to feed his large family.

One of the earlier jobs was shelling pecans. He would bring home a sack of pecans and a nut cracker. One of the family members would crack open the shells. The cracked nuts would be spread across the table and meat of the nut would be separated from the shell and divided into different sizes. Special attention was given to whole pieces because they were worth more. The larger pieces were next and then the smaller pieces. The shelled nuts would be taken to the factory for payment and another sack picked up. The whole process would begin again. The work was tedious and long. Clint often fell asleep when shelling pecans and his mother would send him out to wash his face. This would continue until the family finished up for the night, usually around 8pm. The pay for processing the nuts wasn't much but it paid for food and shelter.

The children would all was their feet before going to bed. They went barefooted all day because the family could only afford one pair of shoes for each child. Which they only wore to school and church.

After some time, Aaren got a job on the WPA. A government project building roads and etc. The year was around 1937 and the family moved to a home on James St. It was not far from the school Clint and Edward attended. Clint was in 2nd grade and Edward was in the 3rd. After a year the family moved to Butler St. Sometime later, they returned to Baxley, GA where life took another turn for the family.

Back in Baxley, the new work was skinning logs, utility poles. You used a hoe like tool to remove the bark off of trees. Father, Edward, and Clint were paid 10 cents a log. Together, they would skin 15 to 20 logs a day. At the end of the week there was enough money to buy the weekly groceries. Which always consisted of a 24lb sack of flour, a peck of meal, sugar, some rice, neck bones, and a piece of fat back. Clint and his brother were always getting into fights. Other kids would tease and ay they wore government overalls. They were probably right.

The family took another means of work by becoming migrant workers. They moved from state to state picking beets and potatoes in South Carolina, String beans in Virginia, tomatoes in Maryland, and potatoes and apples in New Jersey. This also meant living in old houses wherever they went. Often times they shared one room with other families. With only a sheet separating the families. In some cases, they didn't even know the names of the other families.

A bath was once a week in a tin tub. They often had to use the same water to bathe in as their family. So it was always nice to be the 1st or 2nd to wash up.

Everyone worked in the fields from sunrise to sunset. The pay was based on per bushel or basket picked. While in NJ, Clint and his family stayed with his mother's sister for a week. Her name was Ada Harris. Clint's father Aaren had a brother who lived in Philadelphia, PA his name was Joe Hall.

At the end of the harvest season when the family left NJ Clint's Uncle Joe was going to drive them back to Georgia. They got as far as Rocky Mount, NC before the car broke down. From there the family had to take a train to Baxley and Uncle Joe took a train back to Philadelphia. Clint's mother had health issues and only believed in Dr. Branch who practiced in the small town. He gave her medicine for her high blood pressure.

While in Baxley, Clint was allowed to go to work for the "Vegetable Man". This was a man who drove his wagon into town and sold vegetables. Cabbage was 10 cents a head, Beans ten cents a pound, and etc. While staying with them Clint was allowed to eat at the same table even though they were white. They treated him more like a son than a hired hand. At night before going to bed, the "Vegetable Man" would poor out a large jar of coins. This was the money collected from selling his vegetables in town. He would have Clint count them. This was their entertainment before going to bed. During the day Clint would plow the fields. This went on for about two weeks. Then it was time for another move. This time to Florida. Clint was now ten years old.

In Deerfield, Florida the work was to pull tomato plants and pack them into creates. So they could be shipped north. Then it was on to picking string beans and they were paid 25 cents a bushel. This work required crawling on your knees, picking the beans from the bush, and pushing the basket in the dirt ahead of you. One day while pushing the basket ahead of him, Clint's basket began to move. When he tried to make the basket sit upright in the dirt it wouldn't be still.

He stood up and looked over the basket to see what the problem was. The problem turned out to be a large snake. He had placed his basket on top of a rattle snake. Frightened, he screamed out, *"THERE'S A RATTLE SNAKE!!!"* People stopped their bean picking and gathered around. One of the men picked up a stick and killed the snake with it. For the rest of the day, anything that moved was a snake in Clint's mind. Whether it was a bean bush or anything else.

While working and living in Deerfield, FL, the news came that Pearl Harbor had been bombed be the Japanese. This was the start of World War 2 for the United States. At night, all the lights had to be turned off. So there were no street lights on at night.

When string bean picking time was up in this area the family moved to Goulds, FL. One day, Clint's father received a telegram form his sister Angela. The telegram said to come to GA at once because Angela's husband was putting their mother, Clint's Grandmother, out of their home. So back to GA they moved. Clint's father found a house in the country and moved his mother in with them. Grandmother Morning had been born a slave up at "the big house," meaning she was the daughter of the slave owner. She was 12 years old when the slaves were freed and lived with Clint and his family until she passed at the ripe age of 95.

Life as Sharecroppers

After the death of his Grandmother in 1942, the family moved to Tooms County, GA. They lived in an old house and the owner provided 2 mules and a lot of land for the mules to live on. He also had a barn to store food and supplies for the animals.

The family also raised a few hogs. One of the pigs became a pet for Clint's younger brothers Conyer and Frank. When they would lay on the ground the piggy would come snuggle in between them. Edward named his mule Ada. Clint named his mule Joe.

The planting season would begin with plowing the fields and making rows for the tobacco, cotton, corn, and peanuts. The tobacco and cotton were the *money* crops. The corn and peanuts were for animal feed and some personal use. After the growing season, came harvesting time. The tobacco and the cotton were picked. The tobacco had to be cured. After it was picked, it was placed on sticks and hung to dry in the tobacco barn.

The barn contained a furnace. A fire would be started using logs and it was kept burning both day and night. The heat would pass through pipes which were installed inside. The tobacco was hung on sticks and stacked on poles several rows high. The process went on for four days and night and then it was allowed to cool. After it was cured it was placed on croca sheets and taken the market. After harvesting the corn and peanuts, bales of hay were made from the peanut vines. The corn was dried on their stalks and then picked and put in the crib to serve as food for the animals. The family also had a cow named Molly. She produced milk for the family to use.

After a year the family moved back to Baxley to another farm owned by Mr. Mileos. They planted the same crops they had previously. Molly the cow came with them along with a calf so there was plenty of milk. The pet pig came as well but his fate was a little different from Molly's. He wound up being the family's meat source during the winter months.

Another crop was added. It was sugar cane plants. When harvested the juice was squeezed from the stalk by putting it through a grinder which was pulled by a mule. Then the juice was boiled until it became syrup. When it was cooled it was placed in cans. That syrup was so good when it was served with hot biscuits.

At the end of one harvest season Clint's father made enough money to purchase his own mule. The family named him Jake. When you own your own mule you receive a larger percentage of the profits when the tobacco and cotton are sold.

Again the family moved at the end of the harvest season. To another farm in Baxley. It was at this location that one of the saddest things happened in Clint's young life occurred. His mother Eva died.

One morning Clint's mother called him to her bedside. She told him that she was going to the hospital and that she wouldn't be coming back. She was going to deliver her 9th child. Eva said, "Brother, it is what she called him, I won't be coming back home. You have more sense than Jr, aka Edward. I want you to help your father raise these other children. You hear me." Crying Clint begged his mother not to speak that way. His mother was right. She went to Waycross to have the baby and died later that night. The baby lived and was named Audrey.

Clint was 14 years old at the time and the promise he made to his mother placed a heavy burden on him. He worked very hard to carry out his mother's wishes. This burden remained with him even after he got married and began having children of his own.

Life After Sharecropping

Clint's first job after sharecropping was as a dishwasher. He worked at the blue bird café from 7pm to 7am. When he would finish his assigned job washing the dishes he would help the cook. The cook's assistant w very slow. After two weeks the cook made Clint his assistant and the newly demoted assistant washed the dishes. Around 2am, when business was slow, the cook would put some chairs together and then lay down and go to sleep. That left Clint in charge he was 16 years old.

A few months later, Clint got a job at the Ware Hotel as a bus boy and waiter. Various clubs such as the Rotary Club, the Exchange Club, the Lion's Club, and etc. had their meetings at the Hotel and Clint waited on them. He was required to wear a white shirt, black pants, a white jacket, and a bowtie. Clint became so good at waiting tables and serving the club members that often times, some of the club members had him serve in their homes and other places at private parties.

One night when Clint was working at a night club waiting tables the hotel steward came into the club with his friends. Clint waited on them and the steward asked him if he knew where he could find a breakfast cook. Clint replied, "Yes sir, me." The steward told him to report to the hotel by 6am the very next morning.

Clint arrived at the hotel and was expecting to receive training for his new position. However, after he put on his cap and apron and walked behind the counter. The hotel steward said, "There it is," and much to Clint's surprise, he walked away. The first order was eggs benedict. Clint knew about scrambled, over light, and fried but he had no idea what eggs benedict looked like. He asked one of the waitresses named Tiny whom he often carried trays for in the dining room. He struggled until 8am until the other cooks began to arrive. After some direction, he became much better at his job. Some mornings ha cooked up to a crate of eggs, 30 dozen.

At this point Clint had not finished high school. The older women, both black and white, working at the hotel encouraged him to go back and finish his education. When school began he was allowed to move to the evening shift from 4 to 9pm. When school was out Clint was allowed to resume his duties as a breakfast cook. Working from 6am to 1pm. This arrangement continued until he graduated high school.

During his last two years in school Clint along with his buddy Alvin became fishermen and hunters. While fishing they would bait their hooks and then push the handles of their fishing poles into the sand on the river banks, and head down stream to swim. They would play in the water until they would see their poles bending up and down indicating they had a fish on the line. They would jump out of the water and race to the poles and pull the fish out onto the bank. Sometimes it was an eel. They would continue to play and fish until they had good size batch of fish to take home.

As far as hunting went they occasionally caught a rabbit or squirrel. Mostly though they caught raccoons. However, they formed a plan. The raccoons could serve a two-fold purpose. After their hides were dried out they could be sold for 2-3 dollars each. Second, if they were caught alive they could be trained and sold as pets. Both, Clint and Alvin had watched movies of Clyde Beatty taming lions and tigers. So they figured that training raccoons would be a snap! The boys built them a nice cage out of chicken wire but the raccoons didn't cooperate. Needless to say, this plan did not turn out well.

The cage was 8 by 10 feet in size and about 8ft high. A tree was planted inside along with a hollowed out log filled with water. They would catch fish and put them in the log, so the raccoons could fish them out for themselves. They wanted the coons to feel at home. As each raccoon was caught they put a collar around their neck before placing them in the cage. The purpose of the collar was so they could get them out of the cage easier. The boys would take a hook they had made from a clothes hanger reach into the cage and pull the raccoon to the door. Then they would put a chain on the collar and pull the coon out for a walk. For training purposes and to really get attention they would even walk the coons up town. If they needed to go into a store they would simply wrap the chain around a parking meter so the coon couldn't get away.

Finally, they had accumulated 5 female raccoons. If they were going to breed them they need a male. On the last day of the hunting season the boys left school early. They set out to get themselves a male. They decided that the best chance of doing this was in the "government pasture". This was off limits to hunters but they were desperate. Sure enough after a half hour of following barking dogs they spotted a raccoon clinging to a tree. The tree was about 8in deep in water. Clint and Alvin carried spikes designed to climb utility poles. The idea was to climb up the tree behind the raccoon with a switch or stick tucked into their belt. They would then jab him with it until the raccoon jumped out of the tree. Then the dogs would keep his attention until they could climb back down the tree, sneak up on it, and get it into the coon sack.

Getting this one to cooperate was a real hassle. First, he wouldn't jump out of the tree. So Alvin had to climb another tree that was taller. Then punch down at the raccoon until he bailed out of his tree. But the raccoon was a fighter. It took another hour to get him under control enough to get him to the car. Which was about a mile away. Finally, while putting him in the cage we discovered he was the male they had been looking for. Success at last they thought! Little did they realize that this creature would bring their plan to nothing. This raccoon remained in the cage for one night. The next he chewed a hole in the wire fence.

Freeing not only himself but the five females as well. This ended the raccoon for pets program.

The next season they looked everywhere for Lobo, the male raccoon. He had two missing toes indicating that he had been trapped before. They never found him again.

The two of them had worked so hard for months and spent their hard eared money on collars and wire for the cage. And all they had to show for it was the realization that they were no animal trainers.

Oh well on to high school adventures.

Fun Times in High School

In 1949, Clint and his pal Alvin owned a 1946 Chevy. So they were very popular with the girls, not so much with the guys though. There were some advantages of having a car.

Some of the kids from middle school would play hooky and go to the golf course and act as caddies for golfers. The asst. principal, Mrs. Goldy, would send Clint and Alvin over to the golf course to check on these kids and chase them back to school. Clint and Alvin would ask them what their names were, where they lived, and if their parents knew where they were. Then they would pretend to write their names down and tell them to go back to school or else!

Before they owned a car Alvin would at times borrow his father's. But they always had to be back at a certain time. This was thus the inspiration for them to get their own car. Once they were invited to Valdosta, GA to take some young ladies to their senior prom. They caught a ride with some fellow who was going to spend some time with his girlfriend.

After arriving in Valdosta, he allowed them to use his car to pick up their dates and take them to prom. They had a nice time. That is until after they took the girls home at about 1am. They could not find the house where they had dropped off the owner of the car. At that time of night in the 40's and 50's there was not a lot of people to ask information from. So they drove up and down several streets looking for the house. Then the car battery went low and every time they stopped the car or cut the engine off they would have to push it down the road to get it started again. Clint had on his new shoes which were tight. After having danced all night and then pushing the car a number of times to restart it. His feet were sore and hurting. Finally, at about 4am they found the house where they left Jimmy, the owner. They had passed it several times before. Jimmy had to be at work at 7am and they were 60 miles away. Needless to say, despite their explanations this did not sit well with Jimmy. They never got a ride with Jimmy again.

On another occasion, to impress some girls, who happened to be sisters, they rode their bikes 18 miles to Patterson just to see them. The plan was to take the girls swimming in a nearby creek. The girls lived on a small farm about three miles from town. What the boys didn't know was that the girls' father considered Clint and Alvin to be city slickers. He would not the girls out of his sight, not with city slickers. So it goes without saying that they wound up going swimming alone. The girls said they would be along after a while but, that never happened.

On yet another occasion, they caught a bus to see the same sisters. While they were there a fellow delivering furniture, who was from their home town of Waycross, got stuck in the mud. Clint and Alvin helped him get out of the mud. They pushed it and placed sticks and other stuff under the wheels. The man was so thankful that he promised to pick them up later and give them a ride on his way back. He said he would be there around 6pm but he never showed up. Around 8:30pm Clint and Alvin set out to walk the 3 miles to town to catch the 9pm bus. When they arrived the bus had already left. They pondered on what they were going to do next.

Nearby there were railroad tracks with a couple of boxcars on them. They were ½ full with bales of hay. To get away from the mosquitos they made themselves a shelter with the bales of hay. They crawled in and settled down for the night. At around 3am a freight train came by whistling on the next track. It caused them to jump out of their shelters. Sleep was tough to come after that. Near 7am daylight and they got up and walked to the main highway heading toward home. They tried to hitch a ride and got one at about 8am. A man in a pickup stopped and gave them a ride back to Waycross.

Near the end of the school term Clint and his steady girlfriend had a falling out or argument. During the school term she lived in town with her aunt but when school was out she left for home. It was 20 miles away out in the country, (a different direction then the sisters). She would always accuse Clint of seeing other girls. Only half of it was true that's why they had their falling out.

A month after school let out Clint caught the bus and went to see his girl. She lived a couple of miles from the bus stop. When he arrived at her house she asked, "What are you doing here?". So he jokingly replied, "To ask your parents if I can marry you". They were only in the 10th grade. That was the wrong thing to say, because they spent the rest of the evening with her trying to persuade him to go inside and ask her parent. Clint knew he did not intend to ask this from the very beginning. This went on so long that he missed the bus back to Waycross. After walking the two miles to the bus stop he found out he was late. He then had to walk the two miles back to his girlfriend's house. Upon arriving, he knocked on the door and heard someone say, "He's not sleeping in my bed," then the door opened and they let him in. He spent the night and caught the early bus back to town. He had to work at the hotel that morning. It was only two blocks from the hotel to the bus station. And yes, he was late!

Clint and Alvin loved to take their girlfriends swimming in the Satilla River, where they also went fishing. For the girls who couldn't swim they would make a makeshift raft. They did this by cutting down small trees, sapling, and then lashed the small logs on either side of an inner tube which was filled with air. Each girl was placed in and inner tube raft prior to taking off down the river. Clint, who was the strongest swimmer, would go about three to four hundred feet downstream and tie a rope around a tree on one side of the river. Then swim about 150ft across the river and tie the rope around a tree on the other side. The rope hung about a foot above the water. Everyone was instructed that if anyone got caught up in the current, they were to float to the rope grab it, and hang on until help arrived. It turned out that they never had to use the rope. By the way the girls loved it and you guessed it, so did the guys.

Then there was the time Clint and Al headed to Montgomery, AL. Again to see some girls. Al had met his girl about two years earlier when he spent some time in Montgomery. Since they were writing letters to one another Al decided that he wanted to return. He planned to go the next Xmas because school was closed. He wrote his girl to find a girl for his pal Clint. He sent a picture of Clint along with the letter. It wasn't long before Al received a letter back with a picture of a girl inside for Clint. This was a couple of weeks before Xmas. It was still hunting season so they spent the afternoon hunting raccoons before heading to Montgomery. When they got home they washed up and set out for Alabama. It was 10pm and a light rain had begun.

Clint took the first shift and drove. After about 1 ½ hours he became drowsy. Clint told himself that he could make it to the next little town and then he would wake up al to drive and take his turn sleeping. But there was a problem he kept nodding off. Finally, he ran off the road into the ditch. This woke both Clint and Alvin up. Clint continued to drive down the ditch instead of heading into the woods while Alvin was yelling "Clint where are we?!" It took a bit but Clint finally got the car to stop.

As they were getting out of the car, a tractor trailer driver stopped to see if they were ok. He told them he had been blinking his lights for the last half hour in order to keep Clint awake. Apparently, he was driving all over the road. Clint exclaimed, "what lights!?!" Because he never saw any blinking lights. He had indeed been asleep behind the wheel. The tractor trailer driver helped them get back on the road. Alvin took over the driving duties from there. He however, wouldn't let Clint go to sleep while he drove. They discovered they were only about a mile from the River Bridge when they went into the ditch.

They arrived in Montgomery the next morning, tired and sleepy. The girls they were coming to see had planned a party for the evening so they could introduce them to their friends. A party it was! They had real whisky and beer. Clint and Al had never drunk alcohol before. Clint had a beer once when he out with his older brother and his friends, he didn't like the taste of it. Instead of drinking the alcoholic drinks the girls had fixed for them, they would sneak out onto the porch and pour them out. They would then put coke in their cups and sip on that.

The next day the girls were heading to Tuskegee Institute. A group of them were going to put on a play. As well as sing and entertain a group of mentally challenged people. Clint and Al sat in the audience and laughed along with everyone else, and they laughed at everything. What an experience! After the show they went back to Montgomery and the following morning headed home. What a good time they had.

The following spring, they were at the river again doing some wild stuff. They would climb a tree near the river bank and tie a ripe around it. Then find another tree about 20ft further back climb it with the other end of the rope. Then they would do a Tarzan yell and swing out over the river and let go of the rope. It was during this time that he met his wife to be. She was from SC but living with her aunt in GA. They finished high school together in June 1950.

After Graduation

As far back as he could remember Clint had a plan. He planned that by the age of 21 he would have his own home and car. When he graduated in 1950 he had $300 dollars in his savings account. This was a result of saving his tips when he was a waiter and saving a few extra dollars from his paycheck when he could spare it. His Aunt Essie had helped him open a savings account a few years earlier.

After Clint graduated from Center High in June he and Katherine got married that August, not in the original plan. Then he headed north to NJ in October 1950. This was to be a new way of life for Clint.

His first job up north was part time. He worked three days a week in a chicken factory. It was winter and part of his job was to pack the cleaned chicken in boxes of ice to be shipped out. There was no heat in packing area because the ice would melt. Clint's inspiration to work in these conditions was his now pregnant wife who was still back home in GA. In order for him to send for her, he had to have a job.

Every day he looked in the newspapers for another job. It took a while but finally he found one. He went to work in an ice house. When customers came to put their items in he would load it onto a cart and push it into the freezer where it was 30 degrees below zero. When customer came to pick up their things up Clint would go into the freezer, bring their items out, and then load it into their vehicles. It was hard work but it paid $42 dollars a week.

That was $10.00 more dollars a week than working at the chicken factory. He could now send for his wife to join him. Meanwhile, he still looked for a job he was experienced at. Finally, it happened. He got a job at the Woolworth 5&10 Store, in the restaurant, as a busboy. It paid $3.00 less per week but the meals were free and it was a job he had experience in. He and his wife lived with a nice elderly couple they had met at church.

After a few months, Clint received a promotion to making donuts, cakes, etc. This happened because the experienced cooks and bakers were sent to Atlantic City for the summer months because of the increased demand.

Then it happened. The first child, a boy was born two weeks early. They lived about 15 miles from where Clint worked so he had to catch a bus back and forth to work. Clint set out to find a home in town closer to his job. Every place he looked was either a dump or a place he could not afford. One day he saw an ad in the newspaper: A two-bedroom house for sale. $500 down and move in right away. Clint went to see the house and it was in a working class neighborhood. He explained to the broker that he only had $300 at the time but the broker said he would accept it but he had 90 days to get the other $200.00. His mortgage would start now. The mortgage was $45.00 a month and his salary was only $45.00 a week.

Clint would walk the 12 blocks from his job to his house in order to save the 10 cents bus fare. In the meanwhile, the cook at the restaurant quit and Clint asked for his job. This job paid $3.00 more per week. Thanks to a $71.00 tax refund, Clint managed to gather the remaining $200.00 by the time the 90 days were up.

The house had some old furniture, a small table in the kitchen and one chair and an icebox. Clint sat on a milk crate and his wife used the chair. The iceman would deliver a block of ice twice a week. Each delivery cost 50 cents. At work, Clint would bring home the leftovers from the steam table in order to feed his family.

He was now 21 years old and still did not have the car but six months later, before he reached the age of 22 he was able to buy a 1942 Chevrolet. He had reached his goal along with the nice bonus, a family.

Finding a Career

Clint now had a home, a car, and a family. He had one child and another on the way. Still working as, a cook at Woolworths he once again began looking for another job. One that would pay more and provide him with a career.

He asked his insurance agent if they had any openings at his company. He didn't know that the company didn't hire blacks. His wife's insurance agent was black so he asked him if they were hiring agents. He replied, "yes, but you have to be 25 years old." So Clint lied about his age, he told them he was 24. He received and passed the test the test requirements for the job. The district manager of the local office came to Clint's home to inform him he had passed all the tests but there was a problem. His high school records showed his true age. Clint's heart sank.

Clint explained to the manager that because of his age he had a hard time getting a good paying job and all he needed was a chance. The district manager replied, "Well, you are an unusual young man. You already have a home, a family, and seem to be more mature then most young men your age." He hired Clint at the age he had put on his application. Thus began what was to be Clint's life long career in the insurance business.

He started work as a debit agent for Progressive Life. He would have to collect premium payments from people at their homes. Clint also had to find new customers to sell new life insurance policies to. He proved quite successful and seven years later he received his first promotion to staff manager at the age of 29. The job was in Elizabeth City, DC. After a few months he was reassigned to Harbor, MD as a staff manager. At the beginning of his promotion his wife was pregnant with their fourth child so it was agreed that he would not move his family until after the birth of their baby. So while his family was still in NJ, Clint worked and stayed in Harbor and came home on the weekends to be with his family. The result of this situation was not a successful one. Clint decided not to move his family to MD and instead left the company to become an independent insurance agent with Sonnys. This enabled him to write policies for different companies. His office was in Philadelphia, PA, which was across the river from where he lived in Camden, NJ. This job proved to be a good move for Clint. In this position, he could hire his own agents and write policies for more than one company.

After two years of working as an independent agent in Philadelphia, Clint once again began looking for something closer to home. As an independent agent, there was a lot of paperwork involved and he didn't make enough money to hire a secretary. Also, the good agents that he would hire and train would often leave and go to companies that provided benefits and better opportunities.

In 1964, he went to work for a company where he would remain for the rest of his career.

Life at Sonnys Insurance Company

Clint became the first Black agent in NJ to work for Sonnys Insurance Company. This had its own challenges. Starting out once again as a debit agent for Sonnys proved to be a good move for him. He was now working back in the same area where he had started nine years earlier. This meant he already knew a lot of people in the area and this aided in his success. So much so, that his original company tried to get him to come back and work for them once more. When his boss at Sonnys Ins. heard about that, he promoted Clint to staff manager.

The promotion came about in an unusual way.

The agents who worked for his old company Progress Life Insurance began bragging to the agents who worked with Clint at Sonnys, that Clint was going to come back and work for them again. In order to make sure Clint remained with the company, the district manager promoted him.

Clint remained in this position for seven years while white agents with less success were promoted over him. At one point he went on vacation and when he returned he found out that a white agent who only two months before was on his staff, was promoted to being the district manager which made him Clint's boss.

The Regional Manager was about to return to his home state in Mississippi. He held a meeting at a hotel in town. He was a kind man. During his farewell speech he talked about the disappointments in life and the unfair things that happen. After the meeting was over, Egie Smith walked up to Clint, put his arm around his shoulders and said, "Son, you know I was talking to you, don't you? We all know about the injustices in the world and I know you are thinking about quitting. If you left and went somewhere else, it would be the same way. Son, they are not going to make you manager over a predominately White district. But your time will come because you are that good, so be patient son." Those words proved to be helpful to Clint.

In his position as staff manager, Clint had hired and trained several agents, both Black and White. He also conducted all the training classes for the agents to get their licenses in order to sell insurance. The classes were 13 weeks long. Clint remained in this position for seven years and then the "Riots" of the late 60's early 70's broke out across the country including NJ. This would lead to a change in Clint's career.

Clint Becomes District Manager

The company Clint worked for had two offices in NJ. There was one in south Jersey and one in north Jersey. By this time there were several black agents in each office. The district in the north had a lot of problems. Over the course of five years they had appointed five different district managers. All of these managers were white. Some of the problems occurred because the black agents felt their concerns were not being addressed.

They decided to hold out the company's money until their problems were at least listened to. The current district manager called in the regional manager from Philadelphia. That didn't work so they called in the zone vice president, Mr. Lobe. He came from the home office in Peoria, IL. The zone vice president came to the office met with the agents and said, "Now boys, turn in the money and then we'll talk." The black agents insisted that they be heard first. Mr. Lobe then said, "why don't you boys have some lunch and talk it over." When the agents came back from lunch and he asked them what they had decided. Their reply was the same, they wanted to talk first. To this Mr. Lobe stated, "You are all fired!" He then got back on a plane and retuned to Peoria.

When news of the firing was heard in the south Jersey office where Clint worked, the black agents in his office began to rebel. It got so bad that Mr. Lobe had to again fly in from the home office. He first met with the management team. This consisted of the reginal manager, the district manager, and the staff managers. Clint was one of the staff managers.

All of them listened to Mr. Lobe while he tried to justify why he had fired the black agents from the other office. Clint listened for a while and then said, "Mr. Lobe, I have to say this even if it means my job." Mr. Lobe replied, "Go ahead Clint. I know because of your faith; you speak from the heart." Clint began by saying, "Mr. Lobe, I have to go through five or six agents to get one good agent and you come in and fire six black men with a wave of your hand. That is not right."

"I couldn't let them hold a gun to my head." He answered.

"What gun? They can't fire you. You have the gun," Clint said. "I could see suspending them for their insubordination, but firing them? You could have just listened to them first."

"Ah! A suspension... Let's talk about that for a minute," replied Mr. Lobe.

The result was a two-week suspension for the black agents and Clint was sent to the north Jersey office to become the first black district manager, outside of the south side of Peoria. This is where the hard work began for Clint.

Clint the District Manager

The district office that Clint was assigned to was located in a building that was referred to as the lower level but was in fact a basement. The office was quite small. The first thing Clint did was promote two agents to staff manager. One black and one white. Clint had hired and trained the black manager years before in the south office. He also knew the white manager from the previous company he had worked for.

The reginal manager, Alt Farmer objected to promoting the black manager because he had been the leader of the hold out situation. But Clint insisted. The reginal manager then told Clint to write a letter explaining why he wanted to promote, Jim, the black manager.

Clint's letter Stated:

> That this district is a total mess. It is going to take a lot of hard work to straighten it out. That includes Jim. He is a hard worker. I know because I trained him in the business.

The reginal manager finally approved the promotion.

The next step was to hire new agents to fill the open debits. While Clint was servicing one of the open debits himself, he stopped at a bus stop to ask a man where he could find a certain street. The man started to point in the direction of the street, the hesitated and said, "Better yet, I'll show you." With that he hopped into the car. He then said, "Make a left, turn right here." Clint drove for 20 blocks and the man said, "You can let me out here," After he got out the man said, "You can make a right turn here and then make the next right turn and go all the way over until you reach it." At this point Clint realized he had been had. The street he was looking for was only a block from the bus stop. "Hmm, welcome to the big city Clint." He mused to himself. This was Clint's introduction to Newark, NJ.

A couple of months later some of the agents tried to start a union. The company offices in PA were already unionized. This was the result of the company purchasing another insurance company that was already a union co. The home office notified Clint but also told him it would be too expensive to send a company lawyer from Peoria. So Clint was on his own. The company then proceeded to tell Clint what he could and could not say to the agents. Clint asked them to send him enough union contracts and nonunion contracts for each agent, which they did.

Clint held a meeting and gave each agent a copy of both contracts. He proceeded to go through each contract page by page. He already knew the nonunion contract was better. The union contract only made it more difficult to fire someone. Clint then said, "The real issue is determining what kind of manager you have." He then closed the meeting and walked back into his office. The agents went to lunch. About an hour later they returned. The agent who had been appointed leader came into his office and said, "You have nothing to worry about boss. We have you covered."

The next morning was voting time. Management cannot be in the room when the voting is taking place. When Clint returned to the office, what did he see? The leader of the agents, Jones, had a union badge on! Jones then walked into Clint's office laughing saying, "Shook you up didn't I boss. You should have seen your face when you saw the union badge." They both had a good laugh when jones explained the union only received two votes. The home office was happy with the results.

The real work of getting more premium growth for his office began. Premium growth is what determines a district manager's success or failure. By the end of the year, out of over 200 districts, Clint's was top in premium growth. Despite some challenges along the way.

Clint's Office

After eight months of success Clint asked his reginal manager for a new office location. He was told they couldn't afford one. Near the end of the year, the CEO was coming to PA to visit the regional office. The reginal manager told Clint he could come see the CEO regarding a different problem. In the meantime, Clint had a plan. Clint had his cashier, Jean, stand in a puddle of water and he took pictures. Every time there was a heavy rainfall it would flood the office floor. He also took pictures of the old raggedy blinds and the dilapidated furniture.

When he met with the CEO and finished discussing the other problem, the CEO asked him if there was anything else he wanted to discuss. Clint said, "Yes. Here are some pictures of my office." The CEO took one look at the pictures, turned to the reginal manager, and said, "Get him out of there!"

Clint was allowed to find and move into a new office space. His district continued to make progress and over the next six years his district remained in the top 10 districts out of 200 offices in the country. The agency force increased from 12 agents and 2 staff to 33 agents and 4 staff along with 3 cashiers. His district won several awards for outstanding performances.

Clint then made a life changing decision that shocked his company. He informed them he was stepping down from district manager, moving to North Carolina, and would be a field agent. The company thinking money was at stake offered him even bigger offices that would increase his income. Clint made it clear that money was not the issue. He wanted to devote more time to his faith. In October of 1977, Clint moved his family to a place called Mocksville, NC. The town was so small it only had one blinking light in the center of town. Not even a traffic light.

Clint and his family had visited NC several times during the summer vacation months. The family camped out in their recreational vehicle at several campsites. One of Clint's favorite campsites was Tanglewood Park located on route 158 near Clemmons. On one such visit he was shown a beautiful house sitting on a knoll atop 3 acres of wooded land. The home was only 2 years old and unoccupied.

The previous owner was a dairy farmer and had lost his wife some years earlier. His new wife did not want to live on the farm so he built a new house for her. Each morning he would rise at day break and head over to the farm a few miles away and not return until sunset. This had been his custom for many years, working form sunrise to sunset. The new wife could not change that so she finally gave in and they moved back to the farm. Where the farmer again, built her a nice new home.

Before they left NC this time, Clint had bought the home. Clint and the seller agreed that settlement/closing could not take place until December, it was August, because he had to put his home in NJ up for sale. He also had to notify his company of his intentions and train a new district manager.

The Dark before the Dawn

After the move to NC, Clint reported to the company office in Winston Salem. He was once again a debit agent. He was working in this position for about a week when the zone vice president for the southern states, Ellis Lane, visited and asked Clint to accept a staff manager position in the office. This way Clint could keep his company car and remain in management. Clint agreed.

Mr. Lane then informed the Winston Salem district manager that Clint was to receive top pay for this position. Pay was based on salary plus the sale of new premiums produced by the agents on his staff. This arrangement didn't sit well with the district manager because his district wasn't doing well at the time. Clint became his company's first hired black man in management in the state of North Carolina.

Clint remained in this position for two years. However, there was a problem. Clint had not anticipated how this move south would affect his 2 remaining children at home. His youngest daughter had grown increasingly unhappy about the adjustment to the rural way of life. Also Clint's youngest son had managed to tip delicate balance of the south all on his own with dating issues. Hmmm... What to do now? Clint and Katherine decided they would leave the rural life in order to save their family unity.

At a company meeting in Myrtle Beach, SC Clint informed Mr. Lane that he would consider managing a district office again. Mr. Lane asked if he could report that to Charlie, the company CEO. Clint said, "Yes."

A few months later Clint was asked to move to a new house in Ohio. He would be the new district manager in the Lake City office. Clint now face a new challenge, how to fix another troubled district.

Since Clint had responsibilities in his congregation in NC he could not move right away. For seven months he managed the Lake City office during the week and flew home to NC on the weekends. After they found a replacement for him in the congregation he moved his family to Copley, OH. This was another small town. Clint had a method of never moving his family to a large city. He felt a small town was best for raising his children in. His family attended a congregation in Akron. His daughter eventually met and married her husband there.

For the next 2 years Clint managed the office in Lake City. It was a real mess. It had gone "union" a few years earlier. The agents were embezzling the company's money and over charging the policyholders. During Clint's first meeting with the district office staff he informed them that he was aware of their schemes. He reminded them that:

1. It was against the law to steal.
2. It was against company rules.
3. It was against his own personal standards.
4. It was against the law of the God he served.

Then he went on to say, "Here's what's going to happen. I understand that there are a lot of problems here. So for the next 2 months bring me your problems and we will work with them in order to get them solved. After that, we will terminate anyone caught stealing company money or cheating policy holders, union or no union. Some of you have been with this company longer than I have. And you have helped make this company what it is today. We will start with the ones who have the least amount of time with company. If I fire someone who has been here 2 years and you have been here three, then you know you will be next."

Over the next year Clint had terminated so many agents that one came into his office. He said, "Mr. Hill, Clint's last name, I've applied for a loan on my house, so I can pay back the company's money. Clint replied, "You can't come into my office and tell me you stole the company's money because then I would have to terminate you now. And it's not your turn yet. Your turn will come." And it did. Two months later that agents account was audited and he was still short. Despite the loan he had taken out. He was terminated. Next was the union representative's turn to be audited. He too was found short but said he could have money by the next morning. Clint knew in a union, what applies to one applies to all. So he called the home office for permission to allow George, the union rep, to settle his account the next day. Clint knew that the guy who would replace George, if he got fired, was much harder to deal with. The company gave Clint permission to allow George to settle his account the next morning.

Clint also knew where George was going to get the money. He would borrow it from the other agents and then pay them back. In time George again used company's money. This time to pay back the other agents. Three months later Clint had George's staff manager audit George's accounts. Sure enough George was once again short on the money. Clint called him into his office and said, "George you know what I have to do, don't you?" He replied, "Yes, sir. But you know me Mr. Hill, if you had been here years ago, we would all have our jobs. Because our manager was stealing too."

The whole office had accepted Clint and some even said, "Mr. Hill, you are the best manager we ever had." During Clint's time there, the office went from being a total mess to being number 28 out of 200 in premium growth. The agents also decided that they no longer needed a union. This made the company very happy and they decided to move Clint to the home office in Peoria. This began the next step in his career that would lead him to being a company Vice President.

The Home Office

Although, he was now working in Peoria, Clint did not move his family to the big city. Rather they moved to a small town. called Wheaton. It is about 30 miles northwest of Peoria. In the home office Clint was the assistant to the Peoria zone vice president, Bill Martin. Having no specific responsibilities Clint grew increasingly restless and dissatisfied. He was used to running his own operation. Telescope, the holding company conducted an internal audit. The auditors would interview each employee and ask what their duties were. The auditors also asked, "What do you do? How long does it take? Then what else do you do?"

There were over 600 people working in the home office at that time. Clint's daughter Lim also worked at H.O. as an auditor. She audited all field accounts. Since Clint had no specific duties, he asked Bill Martin what was going to happen to him. Bill replied, "The Lord only knows, but wherever I am, you'll be there." By the time the audit was completed over 20% of the work force was without a job. The company set up an office in the hotel down the street in order to assist the ex-employees in finding work elsewhere. For years, that day was referred to as Black Friday among company employees. Clint had not been interviewed.

A few months went by and the company had an outing in Orlando, FL. The CEO was in attendance and Clint approach him with the same question he had asked Bill Martin as well as what Mr. Martin's reply was. Clint then said, "Mr. Donald, as far as this company is concerned, you are the closest thing to the Lord and I want to know what is going to happen to me." Mr. Donald told Clint to call on him on Monday when he returned to the office.

When Clint went to Mr. Donald's office he asked, "Clint how would you like to return to NJ?" Clint became so excited about the prospect of returning home that he wanted to shout but he remained calm and said, "Yes, I would like that." Mr. Donald then explained that the company had been thinking about an expansion plan for NJ. He told Clint to get together with Roy, the company statistician, and put together a 5-year plan. It had to entail how many new district offices could be opened and where, how many new hires would be required, how much annual premium growth would be anticipated and when would the operation become profitable. They were to also address what the market was. This referred to what percentage of the location's population would buy the product, who the competitors were, and what the market expectation for the product was.

It took about two months to put the plan together and present it to the company board. The board approved and Clint was off to handle another challenge that would lead to his becoming a vice president.

In order for Clint to carry out these various assignments and move from place to place, the company would purchase the home that Clint lived in. He would then be transferred to the new assignment where they would provide him with a new mortgage, which would be below the current market interest rates. This enabled him to purchase a home in his new location.

Returning to New Jersey to face a New Challenge

Clint was overjoyed to be back on his home grounds in NJ. At the time, NJ had only two district offices, both of which Clint had worked in and helped establish years before. After several months, he opened a third office in the middle of the state, in Hamilton Township, NJ (near Trenton). An office for him and his personal staff was opened at that location as well.

For a short time, Clint and his wife purchased a home in Willingboro, NJ, while he waited for a house to be built in Mt. Laurel, NJ. This was approximately 20 miles south from where his office was located.

The NJ expansion was going well. There was one big problem though. The zone VP he was now reporting to was a very difficult person to work for.

The CEO had already warned Clint before leaving Peora that this would be a problem. Despite this situation the expansion plan continued to move forward. Clint's title was Regional Manager. His region,1 of 30, led the company in premium growth and by the third year was already profitable. This was achieved in part due to a unique method Clint devised. Two district offices were put in one building with each district manager having his own office. The sales managers and the agents shared the same space but reported on different days.

Instead of having to pay rent on two 2,500sq ft. offices. The cost per square ft. was about 13 to 18 dollars. This method was cost efficient and one of the reasons why the region became profitable before its fifth year. Another reason was each district shared the same cashiers and clerical. So they achieved premium growth with fewer personnel then the original expansion plan called for.

Problems continued with the Zone VP who insisted that everything had to have his approval. Clint had always been able to make his own decisions. For example, he was able to hire whom he wanted, buy what was needed for the office, and etc. This had been true even when he was a district manager. Despite the success of the region he was constantly harassed by the Zone VP. Clint could not deal with the situation any longer. He decided to contact the Mr. Donald with the problem. The CEO then had Clint report directly to him.

After 5 years, the plan had more than exceeded its original goal. Due to its success Clint was one of 3 agency VPs invited to the Telescope office in Los Angeles, CA. He was to meet with and report on the regions progress to the Telescope companies. Sonnys Insurance was the largest of Telescope companies. Telescope was the holding, or parent company, for Sonnys Insurance Company (who Clint worked for) and 51 other companies. Clint had a 15-minute presentation to report his region's success.

All the company representatives were driven back and forth from the hotel to the Telescope Communication office in a white limo (with a bar inside). Clint said to himself, "Abraham Lincoln should see me now. Ha ha!" He had not seen any other Black person from any of the other companies reporting.

This was the peak of Clint's career because a few years later the company decided to downsize but not before Clint was able to achieve another goal which was to move his office within 10 minutes from his home! Because of the downsizing, another change came to Clint's career but not before he had become a vice president.

After 10 years, Clint had assumed that he was in the position where he would spend the rest of his career, but that was not to be.

Clint was now to become vice president of marketing (or marketing director) for the Eastern Area extending from NJ in the northeast to Florida in the south and out to Peora in the west. He was one of four men who had this position and they covered the entire country. Clint was the only Black man.

This position required a lot of traveling. It entailed flying somewhere every week. It also meant having an office in his home with no one reporting to him. His job was to now promote particular policies to assist agents in making more sales. In this position, Clint and his wife could live where ever they wanted so they moved to Wake Forest, North Carolina to build their "dream house."

The new home was on 2 1/2 acres of land. They planted a fruit orchard as well as a large vegetable garden and this made for a happy situation for he and his wife.

The new position was not without its challenges. Clint was now in his 60's and had survived prostate cancer. To ensure success he came up with a new idea. Other marketing directors offered cash rewards to the agents who sold the most policies that were being promoted. Clint decided to use silver dollars in his campaign. This meant ordering thousands of silver dollars. He worked with a bank in NJ who ordered the silver dollars from the federal mint in Philadelphia. Banks don't stock that number of silver dollars at their local branches.

When Clint visited the various district offices he would carry a sack full of silver dollars. He would offer the agents who won prizes to receive their prize money in silver dollars, paper dollars, or a combination of both. This worked so well that soon Clint became known as the "Silver Dollar Man". The district managers would send out requests to, "Send us the Silver Dollar Man." Many of the districts credited their success for the year to the visit of the Silver Dollar Man.

Market Director Challenges

It was now 1992 and Clint now worked in the Casualty Division of his company. Some of the top people in charge hoped Clint would retire due to his age and health issues. How would Clint handle this challenge?

The Marketing directors would visit the district offices which had won awards from the company. Clint, other Marketing directors, and a VP would visit these offices. On one such visit in Oklahoma City, Oklahoma, Clint was given a part on the program. about 15 minutes before the meeting began on a Tuesday morning. This meant that he had no time to familiarize himself with the information before he gave the speech. After the meeting, the three of them caught a flight to Miami, FL. The next day, they were to present an award to a district in Miami, FL. Again, about 15 minutes prior to the meeting began, Clint was given a different part to handle on the meeting and once more he didn't have adequate time to get familiar with his part.

After the meeting, they flew to Greensville, SC and on Thursday they made an award presentation to the district in Greensville. Once more the same stunt was employed, giving Clint a part to handle just 15 minutes prior to the beginning of the meeting.

By now Clint realized, something was afoot and he felt some sort of game was being played on him. When the meeting was over, they all flew back to the home office in Peoria.

On Friday, Clint was called into the office of Bob Slew, the president of the Casualty Division. Bob proceeded to tell Clint that he had performed very poorly on the parts he had been given at the awards presentations in the districts they had visited. Clint responded, "Look Bob, I know what you are trying to do. I'm not going to do anything to get fired and I'll retire when I am ready!" This was one time when being the only Black man in his position was an advantage. No company wants a discrimination law suit especially when over 50% of their business is with that minority group. Clint was also aware that large companies look at people in their 60's or with serious health issues like cancer as a liability. They feel that the employee is not able to carry the work load expected of them.

Although the Silver Dollar Man was still being requested to visit various districts and the Regional Managers of those districts were glad to have Clint make these visits, he felt he should continue to plan for his retirement.

Finally, Clint felt he was in a position to retire comfortably. He and his wife owned their dream home where they had been able to plant several fruit trees as well as pecan trees on the 2 1/2 acres they owned in Wake Forest, NC.

In May, 1995, Clint informed his company of his intentions to retire. They asked him where he wanted his retirement party to be held and he selected NJ where his career had begun some 42 years earlier. At the Hyatt Hotel in Cherry Hill, NJ Clint gave his farewell speech. He quoted from an airline pilot, who had become a professional speech writer, that he had heard speak years before. Clint said, "The one thing I am most proud of is I packed my own Shute." This reference was to the airline pilot who for safety reasons always packed his own parachute and did it his way.

This was really a taunt at those in the company who had wanted him to retire earlier.

One day Clint received a telephone call from Mr. McDonald, the company's former CEO who was now serving as an advisor to the company and semi-retired. Mr. McDonald told Clint that one day he was coming to NC and would tell Clint about the White man's fear of the Black Man. Clint knew what he was referring to. Over the years, there were many things that he had wanted to do with Clint but he could not get approved because of the 'glass ceiling.' A Black man could only go so far in the corporate structure of the White man's world of big business.

Epilogue

Today Clint and his lovely wife Katherine are still enjoying life in there 80's. Looking back Clint see the truth in the Bible he has always put so much faith in. He found strength through his many tribulations.

www.ingramcontent.com/pod-product-compliance
Lightning Source LLC
Chambersburg PA
CBHW021928170526
45157CB00005B/2230